LET'S ROCK

SOIL

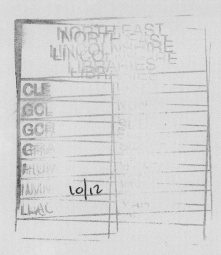

RICHARD AND LOUISE SPILSBURY

Raintree

www.raintreepublishers.co.uk
Visit our website to find out
more information about
Raintree books.

To order:
☎ Phone 0845 6044371
🖷 Fax +44 (0) 1865 312263
🖳 Email myorders@raintreepublishers.co.uk

Customers from outside the UK please telephone +44 1865 312262

Raintree is an imprint of Capstone Global Library Limited,
a company incorporated in England and Wales having its
registered office at 7 Pilgrim Street, London, EC4V 6LB
– Registered company number: 6695582

Text © Capstone Global Library Limited 2011
First published in hardback in 2011
Paperback edition first published in 2012
The moral rights of the proprietor have been asserted.

Edited by Louise Galpine and Diyan Leake
Designed by Victoria Allen
Illustrated by Geoff Ward and KJA artists
Picture research by Hannah Taylor
Originated by Capstone Global Library Ltd
Printed and bound in China by CTPS

ISBN 978 1 406 21912 8 (hardback)
14 13 12 11 10
10 9 8 7 6 5 4 3 2 1

ISBN 978 1 406 21920 3 (paperback)
15 14 13 12 11
10 9 8 7 6 5 4 3 2 1

British Library Cataloguing in Publication Data
Spilsbury, Richard and Louise.
Soil. -- (Let's rock!)
  552.5-dc22
A full catalogue record for this book is available
from the British Library.

Acknowledgements
The author and publisher are grateful to the following for
permission to reproduce copyright material: © Capstone
Publishers p. 29 (Karon Dubke); Corbis pp. 5 (Gallo
Images), **16** (Bob Rowan); istockphoto pp. 6 (© ilbusca), **10**
(© 4kodiak), **14** (© Matt Richard), **15** (© Oksana Perkins),
21 (© Tran The Vuong), **22** (© Luciano Mortula), **23**
(© Ralph125), **27** (© Jonald John Morales); Photolibrary pp. 4
(Garden Picture Library/Francesca Yorke), **8** (Pixtal Images),
9 (Hemis/Patrick Escudero), **18** (Peter Arnold Images/Walter
H. Hodge), **20** (Imagesource); Science Photo Library pp. 13
(Silkeborg Museum, Denmark/Munoz-Yague), **24** (NOAA).

Cover photograph of an eroded cliff reproduced with
permission of Photolibrary (Photoalto).

We would like to thank Dr Stuart Robinson for his invaluable
help in the preparation of this book.

Every effort has been made to contact copyright holders of
any material reproduced in this book. Any omissions will
be rectified in subsequent printings if notice is given to
the publisher.

Disclaimer
All the internet addresses (URLs) given in this book were valid
at the time of going to press. However, due to the dynamic
nature of the internet, some addresses may have changed, or
sites may have changed or ceased to exist since publication.
While the author and publisher regret any inconvenience this
may cause readers, no responsibility for any such changes can
be accepted by either the author or the publisher.

CONTENTS

Rock roles

Find out about the work involved in the study of rocks.

Science tip

Check out our smart tips to learn more about rocks.

Number crunching

Discover the amazing numbers in the world of rocks.

Biography

Read about people who have made important discoveries in the study of rocks.

Some words are printed in bold, **like this**. You can find out what they mean by looking in the glossary on page 30.

WHAT IS SOIL?

Soil is the layer of earth that covers gardens, fields, and other areas of land on our planet. Soil might look like just dirt, but in fact it is made up of several different things.

Soil contains small grains of rock and tiny pieces of natural waste left behind by living things such as leaves. Water and air collect in the spaces between rock grains. There are many animals living in soil, too!

Science tip

Scoop a spoonful of garden soil into a large, clear glass jar and add water. Screw the lid on the jar and shake it. Leave it for a day and watch the soil settle into its different ingredients.

Soil contains substances that could harm you if they get into your mouth. Always wear gloves when working with soil and wash your hands after touching it.

SUPER SOIL!

Soil is one of the Earth's most precious **resources**. We need soil to grow fruit, vegetables, and other plants that people and animals eat. Plants growing in soil also release **oxygen**. Oxygen is a gas in the air that most living things need to breathe to live. Most of us take soil for granted, but we would not be here without it!

In this book we look at the story of soil, how it forms and changes, what lives in it, and how we identify and use different soils.

Plants growing in soil start **food chains**, in which creatures that feed on plants become food for the next animal in the chain. That animal then becomes food for another animal, and so on.

HOW DO ROCKS FORM SOIL?

The first ingredients of soil are tiny grains of rock. Rocks are made from different mixtures of **minerals**. These solid substances do not come from living plants or animals. They form naturally in the earth. **Weathering** breaks large rocks into the tiny grains we see in soils.

CRUMBLING ROCKS

Weathering happens in different ways. For example, smoke from factories and cars contains gases that can mix with rainwater and make it **acidic**. When something is acidic it can damage things. **Acid** in rainwater can dissolve some minerals in softer rocks, such as **limestone** or sandstone. It gradually breaks the surface of the rocks into tiny pieces that start to form soil.

Acid rain can wear away soft rock used for statues, as well as break tiny pieces off rocks on land.

CRACKING OPEN

Weathering can also crumble hard rocks such as **granite** into tiny pieces. If water trickles into cracks in rock and freezes, it expands and takes up more room. As it gets bigger, it forces the cracks open. The small cracks grow bigger and deeper, and the rock's surface gradually breaks up into the small rocks that we find in soil.

This is how ice breaks rock into the tiny pieces, or grains, that start to form soils.

Number crunching

It can take around 100 years for soft rock such as limestone to weather into just 1 centimetre (less than half an inch) of soil. However, it takes up to 10 times longer for hard rock such as granite to weather into the same amount!

Rainwater gets into small cracks in the rock.

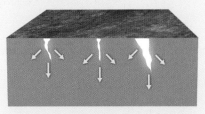

It freezes and expands, causing stresses in the rock which travel outwards. When the ice melts, the crack is a fraction bigger.

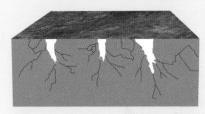

After many cycles of freezing and thawing, the cracks have widened so much that the rock splits apart along these weaknesses.

Eventually, the cracks widen so much that large boulder-sized pieces break from the rock. The process is repeated over and over again.

ROCKS ON THE MOVE

Most soils contain minerals weathered from the rocks they sit on, but other soils contain minerals from elsewhere. Where do these added ingredients come from? Some are carried there by the process of **erosion**. For example, light grains of sand may be blown to new places by the wind. Heavier pieces of rock, such as gravel, may be washed in by rainwater.

Number crunching

On average, soils are about 2 metres (7 feet) deep, but the deepest soils are found in China. These **loess** soils can be up to 400 metres (1,312 feet) deep. They were formed from grains of desert sand that were carried there by winds.

This deep loess soil in north-western China built up over thousands of years as sand eroded from the Gobi Desert.

The plants growing on the slopes of an ancient volcano in Ecuador thrive in soil with added minerals from volcanic ash.

SUDDEN SOIL

Most soils form slowly, but some can change very quickly. For example, new minerals are washed on to surrounding land when rivers flood their banks during strong storms. **Landslides** of loose rock or soil on mountain slopes can **erode** large amounts of weathered rock from one place to another.

In some places, new minerals are added to soil from under the ground. **Volcanoes** are places where hot, liquid rock called **magma** from deep inside the Earth comes out of gaps in the Earth's surface. Sometimes this shoots out of a volcano and then rains down as volcanic **ash**. Ash from volcanoes joins other minerals on land to form a new, rich, dark soil.

WHAT ELSE IS IN SOIL?

Minerals from rocks are just one ingredient of soil. Living things among the grains of rock add ingredients to soil, too.

PLANTS

When plants start to grow among grains of rock, their roots help to bind the new soil together. They also open up spaces for air and water to get in and become part of the soil. Plants take in water, air, and **nutrients** through their roots to help them grow. Nutrients are chemicals that come from minerals and from rotted plant and animal waste.

Science tip

Cut down through soil to see the way plant roots bind it together and make tunnels through the grains of rock. Rainwater and air seep in through spaces like these and become part of the soil.

Plants that grow among rock grains help soils to develop and change.

THE NITROGEN CYCLE

One nutrient that plants need is **nitrogen**. However, most nitrogen is a gas in the air. Living things cannot use it in this form. When tiny living things called **bacteria** live among plant roots, they change nitrogen in air into a form that becomes part of soil. Then plants can use it, and animals in **food chains** can get the nitrogen they need from eating plants. Some of the nitrogen returns to the soil in animal waste, and when the animal dies. Then other soil bacteria change that nitrogen back into a gas in the air – and the whole process begins again.

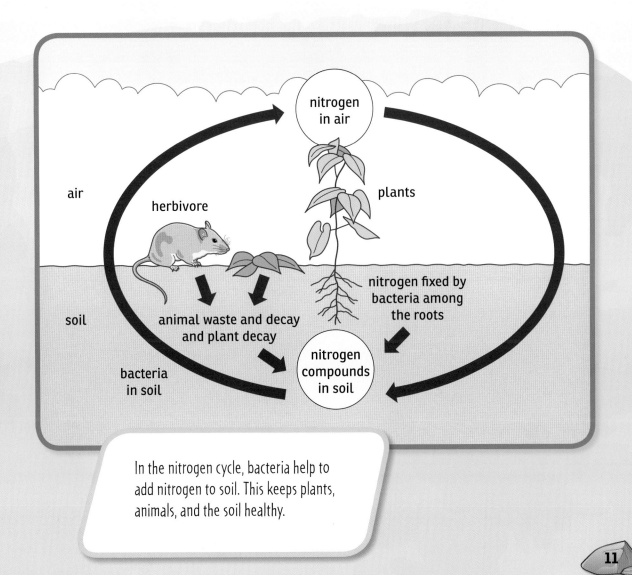

nitrogen in air

air

herbivore

plants

soil

animal waste and decay and plant decay

nitrogen fixed by bacteria among the roots

bacteria in soil

nitrogen compounds in soil

In the nitrogen cycle, bacteria help to add nitrogen to soil. This keeps plants, animals, and the soil healthy.

MAKING SOIL FROM WASTE

As well as adding nitrogen to soil, bacteria and other **decomposers** help to turn waste into another soil ingredient. Decomposers are living things that feed on **organic** matter such as leaves. They break it down into nutrients that plants use to grow. Other decomposers in soil are worms and **fungi** such as mushrooms. Decomposers need water and air to live, so soils low on these ingredients are also low on organic matter and plants.

Sources of organic matter in soil

Plants
- Dead plants and leaves
- Fallen branches
- Seeds
- Withered flowers

Animals
- Dead animal bodies
- Dead skin, hair, nails
- Urine and faeces (waste matter)

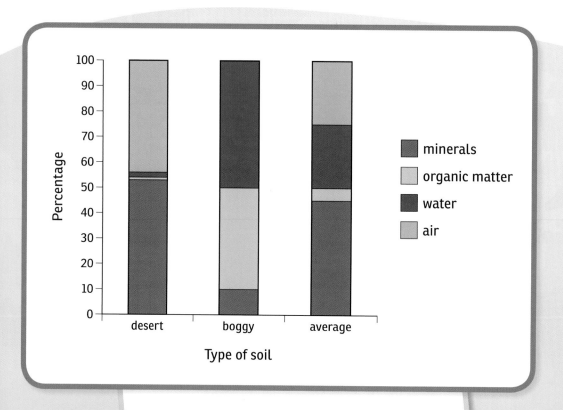

Deserts are low in water and bogs have no air. These soils have few plants because they do not have enough decomposers to break down the organic matter.

WHAT DO DECOMPOSERS ADD TO SOIL?

As decomposers feed on organic matter, they release nutrients from it into the soil. This produces **humus**, the dark, spongy substance that is part of many soils. Humus binds mineral grains together and helps soil soak up water. Plants use the store of nutrients in humus to grow.

Rock roles

Some soil scientists study decomposers to see what they take out of soil, not what they put into it! They study bacteria and fungi to see how they eat and get rid of toxins (substances in soil that can be harmful to living things).

This man was killed and thrown into a Danish bog nearly 2,500 years ago. His body is almost completely intact because boggy soils have few decomposers to rot organic matter.

SOIL ANIMALS

The many kinds of animals that live in (and move through) soil help to create soil and keep it healthy, too. For example, slugs, beetles, and insect **larvae** (young insects) are **scavengers**. They feed on any organic matter they find. Scavengers are messy eaters, and often drop small pieces of organic matter in soil as they feed. These smaller pieces are easy for decomposers to break down.

Science tip

Look for small, coiled piles of soil in a garden. These are worm casts. Earthworms feed by passing soil through their bodies. The wastes they leave behind in casts add nutrients such as nitrogen to soil.

Flies lay eggs on dead animals. The maggots that hatch are scavengers that release small pieces of organic matter into soil.

DIRT DIGGERS

The larger animals that live in or dig through the ground also help to make healthier soils. Animals such as rabbits and prairie dogs dig holes under ground for shelter, or as places to rear their young. Their digging loosens and mixes up the soil and spreads minerals and organic matter throughout the soil. The holes they make also let in more air and water. Animals that graze on plants, such as prairie dogs, also stop land becoming overgrown. This allows a mix of plants to grow, which in turn helps to add a variety of nutrients to the soil.

Prairie dogs dig long networks of tunnels, moving tonnes of soil each year.

HOW DO WE IDENTIFY DIFFERENT SOILS?

Now we know that different balances of ingredients make different soils, we can use colour, **texture**, and other features to identify them.

COLOUR

Most of the many different soil colours are shades of black, brown, red, and yellow, but the colour of soil depends on what it contains. For example, soil rich in **humus** is dark, but soil with few **nutrients** is pale. Soil containing iron **minerals** is often red like rust if it has been draining well, but greyish when it has been too wet for long periods. **Crops** may not grow so well in greyish soils because grey soils are low in **oxygen**.

Scientists note the colour, texture, and location of soils and match them against charts to identify them.

TEXTURE

Another way to sort soils is by texture, which is the way soils feel. Soil texture depends on the size of the rock **particles** they contain. Gravel is the largest of four basic sizes – then sand, silt, and **clay**. There are bigger gaps between big particles, so water and nutrients drain away easily. Clay traps more water but also more nutrients.

Rock roles

Some soil scientists test soils to see how **acidic** they are. This helps farmers and gardeners know what they can grow. Only certain plants, such as heathers, grow well on acid soils. Farmers may add substances to soil to make it less acidic before planting.

Most crops and other plants grow best in soil that has a mix of particle sizes.

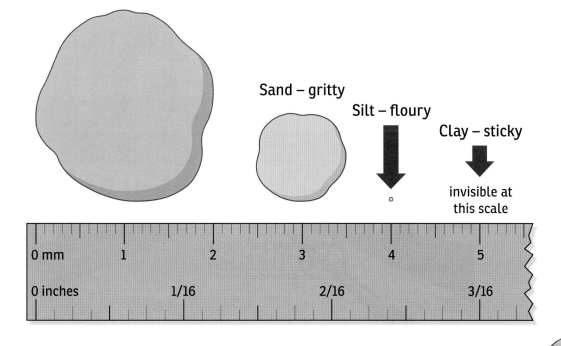

Relative soil particle sizes

Gravel – hard and rough

Sand – gritty

Silt – floury

Clay – sticky

invisible at this scale

0 mm   1   2   3   4   5

0 inches   1/16   2/16   3/16

IN PROFILE

We can also identify soils by their layers. Most soils have four main layers:

- *Topsoil*: the top layer contains the most **organic** matter and humus
- *Subsoil*: contains less organic matter than topsoil, but minerals are concentrated here
- *Weathering horizon*: the layer where bedrock is partly broken down
- *Bedrock*: solid rock that forms the bed, or base, of the soil.

Different soils have different profiles (depths of layers). Prairie soils have thick, humus-rich topsoil because lots of grasses have broken down there over the centuries. Rainforest soils often have thin topsoil that is poor in nutrients because the heavy rainfall there washes them away.

You can identify soil by its profile.

TYPES OF SOIL

Soils vary in many ways. To make things simpler, scientists divide them into different general types. One way to do this is by climate zone.

Each climate zone of the world has its own types of soil. Polar climate zones have podsol and tundra soils. Podsols are light coloured, low in minerals, and generally found in cold forests and moorlands. Tundra soils are found even nearer to the poles. They are dark soils that contain **peat** and are frozen for part of the year. In tropical climate zones, it is so hot and wet all year around that soils are highly **weathered**. These include reddish, mineral-poor laterites and ferralsols which are rich in iron minerals.

Biography

The hobby of the Russian **geologist** Vasily Dokuchayev (1846–1903) was studying and making maps of Russian soils. In the late 1800s, he explained that different soil types existed across the world because of changes in the bedrock material, climate, and living things in different places.

This map shows the location of soil types around the world.

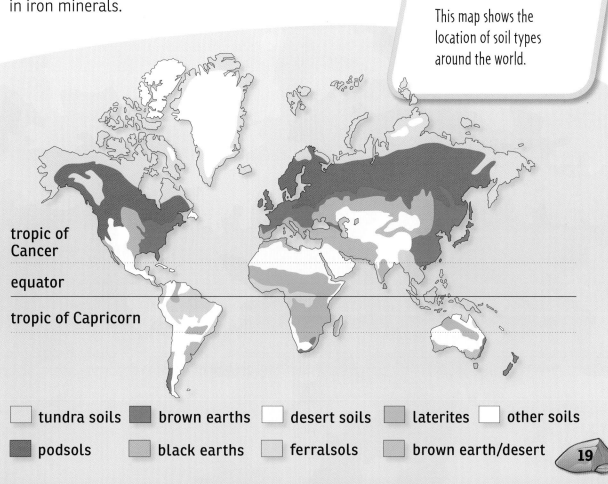

tropic of Cancer

equator

tropic of Capricorn

☐ tundra soils	■ brown earths	☐ desert soils	■ laterites	☐ other soils
■ podsols	■ black earths	☐ ferralsols	■ brown earth/desert	

19

WHAT DO WE USE SOIL FOR?

We use the different soils of the world for so many things that we cannot live without them. We use soils for food, water, building, and even solving crimes!

Plants grown in soil provide drinks, food, clothes, and wood for furniture and many other things. Soil supplies water, **nutrients** from **organic** matter, and **minerals** that **crops** need. For example, **nitrogen** helps leaves grow and **potassium** makes plants resistant to disease.

Rock roles

Forensic **geologists** compare traces of soils found on suspects with the soil at a crime scene. If they match, the suspect probably visited that location and may be guilty of the crime. The first mention of forensic geology was in a story about the detective Sherlock Holmes, in 1887!

How many things in this picture come from plants that grow in soil?

FARMING AROUND THE WORLD

Farmers grow crops all over the world, but what crop grows where depends on the type of soil. For example, rice plants grow best in warm, waterlogged soil that is rich in nutrients. Much of the world's rice is grown in soils in southern India and China that have these conditions.

CHANGING SOILS

Sometimes farmers change soil in order to grow crops in places that do not naturally have the right conditions. They **irrigate** (add water) to dry soils. They add crushed **limestone** rock to **acidic** soil as the minerals in limestone make soil less acidic. They may also add animal **manure** or factory-made **fertilizers** to soil to add extra nutrients for crops.

Farmers all over the world need to have the right type of soil for the crops they want to grow.

SOIL FOR BUILDING

We use soil to make bricks and as a foundation to build on. Soil with lots of **clay particles** is the best for making bricks. The clay stops bricks crumbling, and so makes them stronger. Builders check soils before starting a new house, because buildings sink into clay if it dries and shrinks. Even on firm soils, builders dig down through **topsoil** to **subsoil** that can hold a heavy building.

The Leaning Tower of Pisa in Italy is toppling because it is built on clay soil.

Biography

English soil expert John Burland (born 1936) came up with the idea of drilling out 30 tonnes of dry soil from under one side of the Leaning Tower of Pisa. This side of the tower sank into the wet clay that settled into those holes, making the building a little safer and straighter!

SOIL AND WATER

We use soil to store the water that we need for drinking, cleaning, cooking, and for industries every day. Rain soaks into soil and drains through it to flow into rivers or lakes, and to top up underground water supplies. Soil also filters, or helps to clean, the water as it passes through.

SOIL AND WASTE

We use soil to get rid of rubbish, too. When waste is buried in **landfill sites**, **decomposers** in the soil gradually break down the organic matter in it. Unfortunately, decomposers cannot dispose of plastics, metals, and other waste that is not organic.

At landfill sites like this, decomposers in soil help to get rid of waste that would otherwise form waste mountains all over the Earth.

HOW PEOPLE HARM SOILS

Sometimes, the way people use soils can degrade (damage) them. To clear land for farming, people cut down trees and plants. Without plants to hold soil together, wind and rain can **erode** topsoil. Without topsoil, there are not enough nutrients to grow crops.

In the 1930s, vast areas of land in the central region of the United States were ploughed up to grow crops such as wheat. The area became known as the "Dust Bowl" because the exposed topsoil dried up and millions of tonnes of it blew away in dark storms of dust. Thousands of farmers had to move because they could not grow food on their land.

This picture shows a wall of dust blown up from prairie soils descending on a town in the Dust Bowl during the 1930s.

SPOILING SOIL

Some farmers use soil in a way that keeps it healthy, but some use too many fertilizers to try to make crops grow faster and larger. This harms decomposers in the soil. With fewer decomposers, there is less **humus** and therefore less water and nutrients for crops.

In dry areas, soil can be harmed when farmers dig deep to find more water. If the water they find contains salts from beneath the surface, the salt builds up in the soil and stops crops growing.

Rock roles

Some soil scientists help protect soil. They investigate factories to make sure they are not polluting soil. They use **satellite** cameras to locate places on Earth where soil **erosion** is happening.

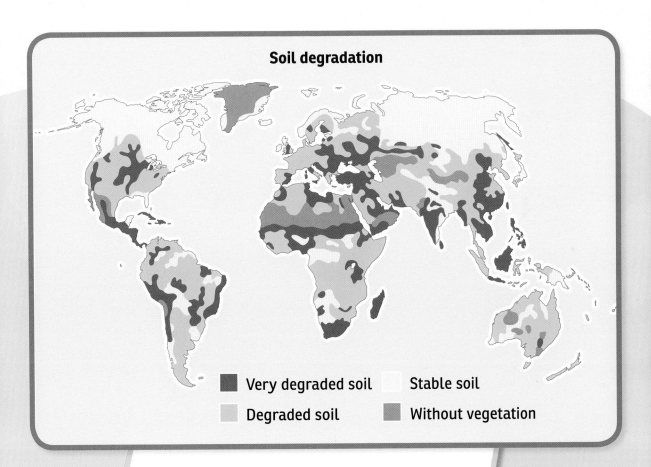

Soil degradation

■ Very degraded soil   □ Stable soil

■ Degraded soil   ■ Without vegetation

Two thirds of world soil is degraded as nutrients have been used up or because it has been harmed by farming.

HOW CAN WE PROTECT SOIL?

Soil is essential for life and takes many years to form, but we have seen how it can be damaged and **eroded** in a very short time. How can we help soil?

We can increase the **nutrients** in soil by adding **organic** matter to the soil around us. Most people produce kitchen and garden waste that can easily be made into compost. **Compost** is rotted organic matter. People make compost by storing organic waste in piles or bins. Compost in soil provides **decomposers** with food and therefore they release nutrients and **humus**. This way of adding nutrients naturally is better than adding chemicals, because it does not risk harming living things in soil.

It is easy to make compost to add to soil and make it healthier.

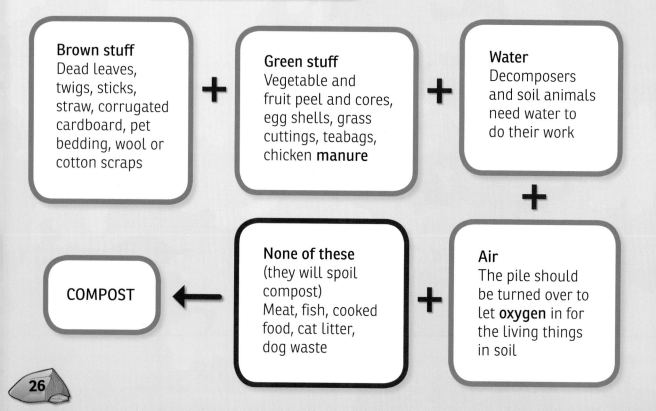

Brown stuff
Dead leaves, twigs, sticks, straw, corrugated cardboard, pet bedding, wool or cotton scraps

+

Green stuff
Vegetable and fruit peel and cores, egg shells, grass cuttings, teabags, chicken **manure**

+

Water
Decomposers and soil animals need water to do their work

+

Air
The pile should be turned over to let **oxygen** in for the living things in soil

+

None of these
(they will spoil compost)
Meat, fish, cooked food, cat litter, dog waste

← **COMPOST**

STOPPING EROSION

People stop soil **erosion** in different ways. They plant trees and hedges next to farmland to block winds that can blow **topsoil** away. Farmers plough across rather than down slopes to stop rainwater from washing soil away. Gardeners can buy compost that doesn't use **peat** taken from rare bog soils.

The story of soil is a fascinating one. Next time you step outside, spare a thought for the soils beneath our feet and what they do for us!

Biography

In 1976, the Kenyan scientist Wangari Maathai (1940–2011) started a movement to plant trees, partly to reduce soil erosion. Now 40 million trees have been planted in Kenya and the aim is to plant 1 billion trees worldwide!

Farmers build terraces on slopes to stop soil erosion and to store water in soil so they can grow rice.

MAKE A DIRT SHIRT!

The coloured **minerals** in soil can be used to dye a T-shirt.

YOU WILL NEED:
- an apron
- an old bucket
- a measuring jug
- washing soda
- a clean, dry, white cotton T-shirt
- rubber gloves
- 1 kg (2 lb) soil (brightly coloured soil is best)
- an old wooden spoon
- vinegar
- a cup

WHAT TO DO:

1 Put on the apron – you could get wet or muddy!

2 Add 3 litres (6 pints) of cold water to the bucket with half a cup of washing soda. (It will help the T-shirt soak up colour.) Stir to mix. Put the T-shirt in the bucket for one hour.

3 Squeeze out the T-shirt and leave on one side. Wearing gloves, add soil to the bucket with 8 litres (16 pints) of hot tap water to make thin mud. Stir with the wooden spoon. Add one cup of vinegar to help the mineral colours move from the mud into the cloth.

4 Leave the T-shirt to soak in the mud for four hours. Stir it now and again to make sure all parts are soaked in the mud.

5 Rinse the cloth gently in cold water in a sink to get rid of rock **particles**. Hang it up to dry. Then wash it on a cold cycle in a washing machine. Dry it somewhere warm, such as a hot tumble drier, before wearing it.

Science tip

Tie knots in the T-shirt using rubber bands before you dye it, to create a tie-dye dirt shirt with different patterns. Make the colour darker by repeating the process several times.

GLOSSARY

acid substance, usually liquid, that can damage things it touches if very strong

acidic contains acids

ash grey or black powder that is left after something has burnt

bacteria simple and tiny living things that live in water, air, soil, and other living things

bedrock layer of solid rock beneath soil and sand

clay soil with very fine grains

compost rotted organic matter

crop plant that people grow large amounts of, usually for food

decomposer something that breaks down and rots materials such as waste

dissolve completely mix with a liquid

erode wear away

erosion wearing away of rocks by flowing water, wind, and glaciers

fertilizer substance that farmers put on soil to make plants grow larger and faster

food chain way of showing the feeding relationships among living things

fungi living things such as mushrooms that usually grow in soil and feed on decaying matter

geologist scientist who studies the rocks and soil from which the Earth is made

granite type of hard rock often used in building

humus dark organic material in soils produced by the breaking down of plant and animal matter

irrigate to add water to soil to help plants grow

landfill site place where waste is disposed of by burying it under ground

landslide mass of rock or soil sliding down a slope

larvae young form of insects, such as caterpillars or maggots

limestone rock made up of the mineral calcite, which can come from the shells and skeletons of sea animals

loess soil made up of small particles that were carried there by the wind

magma molten rock below the Earth's crust

manure waste matter (dung) from animals that is mixed with soil to help plants grow

mineral non-living substance that is naturally present in the earth, such as gold and salt

nitrogen chemical that living things need but that mostly exists as a gas in the air

nutrient substance that living things need to stay alive and to grow

organic produced by or from living things

oxygen gas in the air that living things need in order to live

particle very tiny piece of something

peat soft black or brown substance that forms from rotting plant matter

potassium substance that is found in soil and that plants use to stay healthy

resource supply of something that people need and use, such as water, soil, or oil

satellite electronic device that is sent into space and moves around the Earth

scavenger animal that eats waste or dead animals killed by other animals

subsoil layer of soil below topsoil that contains less organic matter than topsoil, but more minerals

texture the way something feels, such as crumbly or sticky

topsoil top layer of soil that contains the most organic matter and humus

volcano opening in the Earth's surface where magma escapes from under ground

weathering breaking up of rock by weather conditions such as extremes of temperature

weathering horizon lowest soil layer where bedrock is partly broken down

FIND OUT MORE

BOOKS

100 Rocks and Minerals to Spot (Usborne Spotter's Cards), Philip Clarke (Usborne, 2008)

Rocks and Soil (Investigate), Sue Barraclough and Charlotte Guillain (Heinemann Library, 2008)

Soil (Geology Rocks!), Rebecca Faulkner (Raintree, 2008)

Vitamins and Minerals for a Healthy Body (Body Needs), Angela Royston (Heinemann Library, 2009)

WEBSITES

Do you want to know more about decomposers and other tiny living things in soil? Check out: **commtechlab.msu.edu/sites/dlc-me/zoo/zdmain.html**

You might be interested in the range of jobs soil scientists do at: **soils.usda.gov/education/facts/careers.html**

Help Detective Le Plant find clues in soil! Visit: **urbanext.illinois.edu/gpe/case2/index.html**

Do you need some more instructions for making compost? Try: **www.dnr.state.wi.us/org/caer/ce/eek/earth/recycle/compost_waste.htm**

INDEX